John James Piatt

Poems in Sunshine and Firelight

John James Piatt

Poems in Sunshine and Firelight

ISBN/EAN: 9783337256289

Printed in Europe, USA, Canada, Australia, Japan

Cover: Foto ©Thomas Meinert / pixelio.de

More available books at **www.hansebooks.com**

POEMS

IN

SUNSHINE AND FIRELIGHT.

BY

JOHN JAMES PIATT.

CINCINNATI:
R. W. CARROLL & CO.,
73 WEST FOURTH STREET,
OPERA-HOUSE BUILDING.
1866.

To E. C. S.

———•———

I DEDICATE THIS BOOK, DEAR FRIEND, TO YOU—
   KNOWING YOUR OTHER FRIENDS, A HOST UNSPOKEN,
WILL SAY: "TO ONE SO BRIGHT, SO WARM, SO TRUE,
   OUR HEARTS SHOULD BEAR HOW MANY A WORTHIER TOKEN!"

J. J. P.

WASHINGTON, D. C., December, 1865.

CONTENTS.

	PAGE
DEDICATION	3
The Pioneer's Chimney	9
Reading the Milestone	20
The Mower in Ohio	21
The Sunshine of Shadows	26
Higher Tenants	28
Passengers	31
Sundown	33
The Old Man and the Spring-Leaves	35
Fires in Illinois	38
King's Tavern	41
One of Two	44
At Evening	45
A Lost Graveyard	47
The Sight of Angels	49
Taking the Night-Train	50
To the Lares	52
Outgoing	53
To a Child	56
In October	57
White Frost	58
Resurrection	59
Foresight of Fate	62
To my Brother Guy	63
To One in a Darkened House	66
The Blue-Bird's Burial	67
Sleep	71
Firelight Abroad	72
The Buried Ring	75
The White Lily	77
Twofold	78
Anniversary	79
Awake in Darkness	80
For a Gravestone	81

CONTENTS.

FOOTSTEPS RETURNING.

	PAGE
Riding the Horse to Market	85
"To ———"	90
After a While	92
Genius Loci	94
Melancholy	96
The Week	97
Folded Down	98
Mirage	101
An Echo	102
September	103
Fallen Leaves	104
Travelers	106
The Love-Letter	107
Confidants	108
The Birds of Longing	109

FIVE YEARS.

Honors of War	113
The Ballad of a Rose	115
The Open Slave-Pen	119
Riding to Vote	122
The Unbended Bow	126

SUNSHINE AND FIRELIGHT.

THE PIONEER'S CHIMNEY.

WE leave the highway here a little space—
(So much of life is near so much of death:)
The chimney of a dwelling still is seen,
A little mound of ruin, overgrown
With lithe, long grasses and domestic weeds,
Among the apple-trees (the ancestors
Of yonder orchard fruited from their boughs)—
The apple-trees that, when the place was rough
With the wild forests, and the land was new,
He planted: one, departed long ago,
But still a presence unforgotten here,
Who bless'd me in my boyhood, with his hands
That seem'd like one's anointed. Gentle, strong,
And warm'd with sunny goodness, warming all,
Was he, familiar by the reverend name
Of Uncle Gardner in our neighborhood:
His love had grown to common property
By ties that Nature draws from man to man,
And so at last had claim'd the bond of blood.

THE PIONEER'S CHIMNEY.

He was an elder in the land, and held
His first proprietary right, it seem'd,
From Nature's self; for, in an earlier day,
He came with others, who of old had reach'd
Their neighbor hands across New England farms,
Over the mountains to this Western Land—
A journey long and slow and perilous,
With many hardships and the homesick look
Of wife and children backward; chose his farm,
Builded his house, and clear'd, by hard degrees,
Acres that years ago were meadows broad,
Or wheat-fields rocking in the summer heat.

His children grew, and son and daughter pass'd
Into the world that grew around, and some
Into that world which evermore unseen
Is still about us, and the graveyard where
Their bodies slept (a few half sinking stones,
A stranger's eyes would hardly see them, show
Seventy rods yonder in the higher ground)
Gave still a tenderer title, year by year,
To the dear places earn'd by earlier toil.

Meanwhile the years that made these woody vales
An eager commonwealth of crowding men

THE PIONEER'S CHIMNEY.

Pass'd, one by one, and every thing was changed;
And he, whose limbs were like the hickory's when
He came with life's wrought vigor here, was changed:
He heard the voice that tells men they are old.
Yet not the less he moved his usual rounds,
Walk'd his old paths; not idle, sweated still
With scythe or sickle in the hay or wheat;
Follow'd his plow when in the April sun
The blackbird chatter'd after and the crow
Far-off look'd anxious for the new-dropp'd corn;
And gave the winter hours their services,
With sheep abroad on slopes that, slanting south,
Breathe off the snow and show a warming green,
With cattle penn'd at home or bounding flail:
So, not forgetting social offices
Throughout all seasons, (gaining so the love
That went acknowledged in his common name,)
He, like the Servant in the Parable,
Doing his duty, waited for his Lord.

The chimney shows enough for memory,
And, it may be, a stranger passing close,
If thoughtful, well might think a tender thought
Of vanish'd fireside faces, in his dream
Suddenly lighted by a vanish'd fire.

And should the apple-trees that linger, loth
To end their blossoming, attract his eye,
Their fragrance would not pass unrecognized
For deeper gifts than fragrance. He is gone
Who planted them, and thirty years are gone.
Now, if you look a quarter-mile away,
Beyond the toll-gate and its lifted sweep,
You see a prouder house—not new nor old—
Beneath whose later roof no spirit dwells
That had its tenure here: a stranger holds
The secondary ownership of law.

It is a story, common though it seem,
Tender and having pathos for the heart
Which knows, but will not know, that he who says
"My own," and looks to-day on willing fields,
And sets his family tree in trusted ground,
To-morrow hears another answer "Mine."
Listen; if you will listen. It is hard
To go an alien from familiar doors
When we are young, to wrestle where we go,
And win or lose exulting—we are strong;
But it is pitiful when weak and old,
When only for the near in life we seek,

And heaven, yearn'd after, is not thought of far,
To lose our shelter and to want for rest.

Of Uncle Gardner's children three were dead—
Yonder they lie. Their mother and two with him
(Two youngest: one a boy of fourteen years,
His latest child—a girl three years beyond)
Breathed in his close, contented atmosphere;
An elder daughter, wedded years before,
Lived far away in watery Michigan;
His eldest son—and the first-born of all—
Thrived as a merchant in the city near,
Had thriven, at least, or so 'twas said, and he
For some keen chance had got the old man's will
To be his bond. The father pledged the land—
Willing for the grown man, yet for the boy
And for his girl at home regretfully,
Deeming the chance a rash one. From that day
He wrought his daily labors ill-content,
And with a trouble in his countenance,
That would not put a false face on his heart.
To things familiar came a subtle change.
The brook that long ago, companion-like,
Had grown acquainted with his solitude,
And, later, made him music when he walk'd

THE PIONEER'S CHIMNEY.

And led his children through the pasture-ground
Up to the haying or the harvest-gap,
A noisy mimic of their prattled words,
Now seem'd to lift a stranger's face at him,
Wondering why he came there, who he was,
Or murmur'd, with a long and low lament,
Some undercurrent of an exile's song
That is not on his lips but in his heart.
Nothing was as it had been: something vague,
That Present of the Future which is born
Within the bosom, whispering what will be,
Met him and follow'd him, and would not cease
To meet and follow him: it seem'd to say
"The place that knew you shall know you no more."
And oftentimes he saw the highway stirr'd
With slowly-journeying dust, and, passing slow,
The many who forever in our land
Were going farther, driven by goads unseen,
Or not content and looking for the new;
And then he thought of how in those dear days
He, too, had ventured, and again he saw
With steadfast eyes forgotten faces, known
When he was young, and others dear to him
From whom he parted with regret but firm
In the strong purposes which build the world;

Thought of his consolation—she most dear
Was with him, they most helpless with him, too,
For whom he sought a newer world of hope:
"But I am old," he murmur'd, "she is old,"
And saw his hand was shaken like his thought.

Such were his troubled fancies. When he slept,
In his slow dreams—with lagging team, the last
Of many that in yonder meadows foal'd
Grew and became a portion of the place—
Journeying far away, and never more
Reaching his journey's goal, (a weary road
Whose end came only with the waking day.)
He seem'd to pass, and always 'twas the same:
Through new-built villages of joyous homes,
Homes not for him, by openings recent-made,
But not for him, by cultivated farms
Of other men—and always 'twas the same.
Then, when he woke and found the dream a dream,
And through his window shone the sun and brought
The faint rich smell of the new-tassel'd corn,
More fragrant from the dew that weigh'd it down,
He murmur'd of his fields—"For other men;
They are not mine. The mortgage will be closed;
The mortgage goes wherever I shall go."

So pass'd the quarter of a year, and so
The old man, burden'd with his little world,
Felt it upon his shoulders, stooping down,
Bent more with this than every other year.
And summer pass'd to autumn: in his door
He sat and saw the leaves, his friends of old,
Audible in the sunshine, falling, falling,
With a continuous rustle—music fit
For his accompanying thought. At last it came,
The blow that reach'd his heart before it came,
For all was lost: the son whose risk he placed
Both on his children's home and on his heart
Was ruin'd, as the careless worldlings say—
Ruin'd indeed, it seem'd, for on his brain
The quick stroke flash'd: for many years the son
Breathed in a world in which he did not live.

The old man took the blow but did not fall—
Its weight had been before. The land was sold.
The mortgage closed. That winter, cold and long,
(Permitted by the hand that grasp'd his all
That winter pass'd he here,) beside his fire,
He talk'd of moving in the spring, he talk'd
(While the shrill sap cried in a troubled blaze)
Like one whose life was not all broken down,

THE PIONEER'S CHIMNEY.

Cheerfully garrulous, with words that show
False witnesses of hope and seeming strength
When these are gone and come not. In the spring,
When the first warmth had brooded every-where,
He sat beside his doorway in that warmth,
Watching the wagons on the highway pass,
With something of the memory of his dread
In the last autumn; and he fell asleep.
Perhaps within his sleep he seem'd again
Journeying far away for evermore,
Leaving behind the homes of other men,
Seeking a newer home for those he loved,
A pioneer again. And so he slept—

And still he sleeps: his grave is one of those.

His wife soon joined his sleep beside him there.

Their children Time has taken and the world.

The chimney shows enough for memory,
The graves remain; all other trace is gone,
Except the apple-trees that linger, loth
To end their blossoming. In restless moods
I used to wander hither oftentimes,

And often linger'd till the twilight came,
Touch'd with the melancholy breathed by change;
And something in the atmosphere, I thought,
Remain'd of hours and faces that had been.
Then, thinking of the Past and all I knew
And all remember'd of it—most of him
Whose vanish'd fireside blazed so near me here—
My fancy, half unconscious, shaped the things
Which had been, and among the quiet trees
The chimney from its burial mound arose;
The ruin'd farm-house grew a quiet ghost—
Its walls were thrill'd with murmur-music, humm'd
By inner voices scarcely heard without;
And from the window breathed a vaporous light
Into the outer mist of vernal dark,
And lo! a crowd of sparks against the sky
Sprang suddenly, at times, and from the wood
(The wood?—no wood was here for forty years!)
Bark'd the shrill fox and all the stars hung bright.
Till, busy with the silence far away,
(And whether heard or heard not hardly known,)
First indistinct, then louder, nearer still,
And ever louder, grew a tremulous roar;
Then, sudden, flared a torch from out the night,
And, eastward half-a-mile, the shimmering train

THE PIONEER'S CHIMNEY.

Hurried across the darkness and the dream,
And all my fantasy was gone, at once—
The lighted window and the fireside sound:
I saw the heap of ruin underfoot,
And overhead the leaves were jarr'd awake,
Whispering a moment of the flying fright,
And far away the whistle, like a cry,
Shrill in the darkness reach'd the waiting town.

READING THE MILESTONE.

I stopp'd to read the Milestone here,
    A laggard school-boy, long ago;
I came not far—my home was near—
    But ah, how far I long'd to go!

Behold a number and a name,
    A finger, Westward, cut in stone:
The vision of a city came,
    Across the dust and distance shown.

Around me lay the farms asleep
    In hazes of autumnal air,
And sounds that quiet loves to keep
    Were heard, and heard not, every-where.

I read the Milestone, day by day:
    I yearn'd to cross the barren bound,
To know the golden Far-away,
    To walk the new Enchanted Ground!

THE MOWER IN OHIO.

JUNE, MDCCCLXIV.

The bees in the clover are making honey, and I am making my hay:
The air is fresh, I seem to draw a young man's breath to-day.

The bees and I are alone in the grass: the air is so very still
I hear the dam, so loud, that shines beyond the sullen mill.

Yes, the air is so still that I hear almost the sounds I can not hear—
That, when no other sound is plain, ring in my empty ear:

The chime of striking scythes, the fall of the heavy swaths they sweep—

They ring about me, resting, when I waver half
    asleep;

So still I am not sure if a cloud, low down, unseen
    there be,
Or if something brings a rumor home of the cannon
    so far from me:

Far away in Virginia where Joseph and Grant, I know,
Will tell them what I meant when first I had my
    mowers go!

Joseph he is my eldest one, the only boy of my three
Whose shadow can darken my door again, and lighten
    my heart for me.

Joseph he is my eldest—how his scythe was striking
    ahead!
William was better at shorter heats, but Jo in the
    long-run led.

William he was my youngest; John, between them,
    I somehow see,
When my eyes are shut, with a little board at his
    head in Tennessee.

But William came home one morning early, from Gettysburg, last July
(The mowing was over already, although the only mower was I:)

William, my captain, came home for good to his mother; and I'll be bound
We were proud and cried to see the flag that wrapt his coffin around;

For a company from the town came up ten miles with music and gun:
It seem'd his country claim'd him then—as well as his mother—her son.

But Joseph is yonder with Grant to-day, a thousand miles or near,
And only the bees are abroad at work with me in the clover here.

Was it a murmur of thunder I heard that humm'd again in the air?
Yet, may be, the cannon are sounding now their Onward to Richmond there.

THE MOWER IN OHIO.

But under the beech by the orchard, at noon, I sat
    an hour it would seem—
It may be I slept a minute, too, or waver'd into a
    dream.

For I saw my boys, across the field, by the flashes
    as they went,
Tramping a steady tramp as of old with the strength
    in their arms unspent;

Tramping a steady tramp, they moved like soldiers
    that march to the beat
Of music that seems, a part of themselves, to rise
    and fall with their feet;

Tramping a steady tramp, they came with flashes of
    silver that shone,
Every step, from their scythes that rang as if they
    needed the stone—

(The field is wide and heavy with grass)—and, com-
    ing toward me they beam'd
With a shine of light in their faces at once, and—
    surely I must have dream'd!

For I sat alone in the clover-field, the bees were working ahead.
There were three in my vision—remember, old man: and what if Joseph were dead!

But I hope that he and Grant (the flag above them both, to boot,)
Will go into Richmond together, no matter which is ahead or afoot!

Meantime alone at the mowing here—an old man somewhat gray—
I must stay at home as long as I can, making myself the hay.

And so another round—the quail in the orchard whistles blithe—
But first I'll drink at the spring below, and whet again my scythe.

THE SUNSHINE OF SHADOWS.

ON A PHOTOGRAPH OF THREE CHILDREN.

THREE children's shadow-faces look
From my familiar picture-book:
Far from their father's threshold sweet
I found them in a noisy street.

"Dear children, come with me," I said,
"And make my home your own instead;
Your gentle looks, your tender words,
Shall mate the sunbeams, charm the birds."

They came, but never lip is stirr'd
With merry laugh or mirthful word:
As in a trance at me they look
Whene'er I ope their prisoning book.

But as I gaze, in revery bound,
The silence overflows with sound:

THE SUNSHINE OF SHADOWS.

From garden haunts of birds and bees
Hum voices through the blossoming trees.

Like waters heard when breezes blow,
Light laughters waver to and fro;
Then, when my dream is gone, I say
"Some wind has blown the sound away."

For the light breeze, alighting brief,
Turns with its sudden wings the leaf,
And, like a passing sunshine, they
Seem so to shout and fly away!

HIGHER TENANTS.

After Winter fires were ended, and the last spark, vanishing
From the embers on our hearthstone, flew into the sky of spring:

In the night-time, in the morning—when the air was hush'd around—
Throbbing vaguely on the silence, came a dull, mysterious sound:

Like the sultry hum of thunder, at the sullen close of day,
Out of clouds that brood and threaten on the horizon far away.

"'T is," I said, "the April thunder," and I thought of flowers that spring,
And of trees, that stand in blossom, and of birds that fly and sing.

But the sound, repeated often—nearer, more familiar grown—
From our chimney seem'd descending, and the swallow's wings were known.

Where the lithe flames leap'd and lighten'd, charm of host and cheer of guest,
There the emigrant of Summer chose its homestead, built its nest.

Then I dream'd of poets dwelling, like the swallow, long ago,
Overhead in dusky places ere their songs were heard below;

Overhead in humble attics, ministers of higher things:
Underneath were busy people, overhead were heavenly wings!

And I thought of homely proverbs that on simple lips had birth,
Born of gentle superstitions at old firesides of the earth:

How, where'er the swallow builded under human
    roofs its nest,
Something holier, purer, higher, in the house became
    a guest;

Peace, or Love, or Health, or Fortune—something
    Prosperous, from the air
'Lighting with the wings of swallows, breathed
    divine possession there.

"Friendly gods," I said, "descending, make their
    gentler visits so,
Fill the air with benedictions—songs above and
    songs below!"

Then I murmur'd, "Welcome, swallow; I, your land-
    lord, stand content:
Even if song were not sufficient, higher Tenants pay
    your rent!"

PASSENGERS.

Night held aloft the gentle star,
    Her earliest watchfire in the dark,
And by the window of the car
    Flutter'd and flew the hurrying spark.

Its pathway finding through the snows,
    The train rush'd on with tremulous roar—
Like one whose purpose burns and glows,
    A torch to lead his life, before.

The darkness grew around the face
    Of every traveler for the night:
A sudden vision fill'd the place
    And touch'd the gloom with tender light.

Not from the holy world unknown:
    A gentle mission of the air
From happy hearth and threshold flown,
    Familiar angels, gather'd there.

O prayers that breathe from faces bright,
  O thoughts of love that will not sleep,
O dreams that give the soul by night
  Its wings the body may not keep!

Not unattended, far away,
  The wanderer moves with throngs unknown;
Ye meet or follow, night or day—
  I saw your heavenly shapes alone!

SUNDOWN.

While stealthy breezes kiss to frosty gold
   The swells of foliage down the vale serene,
      And all the sunset fills
      The dreamland of the hills,
Now all the enchantment of October old
   Feels a cold veil fall o'er its passing scene.

Low sounds of Autumn creep along the plains,
   Through the wide stillness of the woodlands brown,
      Where the still waters glean
      The melancholy scene;
The cattle, lingering slow through river lanes,
   Brush yellowing vines that swing through elm-trees down.

The forests, climbing up the northern air,
   Wear far an azure slumber through the light,
      Showing, in pictures strange,
      The stealthy wand of change;
The corn shows languid breezes, here and there—
   Faint-heard o'er all the bottoms wide and bright.

SUNDOWN.

On many a silent circle slowly blown,
    The hawk, in sun-flush'd calm suspended high,
        With careless trust of might
        Slides wing-wide through the light—
Now golden through the restless dazzle shown,
    Now drooping down, now swinging up the sky.

Wind-worn along their sunburnt gables old,
    The barns are full of all the Indian sun,
        In golden quiet wrought
        Like webs of dreamy thought,
And in their Winter clasp serenely fold
    The green year's earnest promise harvest-won.

With evening bells that gather, low or loud,
    A village, through the distance, poplar-bound,
        O'er meadows silent grown,
        And lanes with crisp leaves strown,
Lifts up one spire, aflame, against a cloud
    That slumbers eastward, slow and silver-crowned.

THE OLD MAN AND THE SPRING-LEAVES.

Underneath the beechen tree
All things fall in love with me!
Birds, that sing so sweetly, sung
Ne'er more sweet when I was young;
Some sweet breeze, I *will* not see,
Steals to kiss me lovingly;
All the leaves, so blithe and bright,
Dancing sing in Maying light
Over me: "At last, at last,
He has stolen from the Past."

Wherefore, leaves, so gladly mad?
I am rather sad than glad.

"He is the merry child that play'd
Underneath our beechen shade,
Years ago; whom all things bright
Gladden'd, glad with his delight!"

THE OLD MAN AND THE SPRING-LEAVES.

I am not the child that play'd
Underneath your beechen shade;
I am not the boy ye sung
Songs to, in lost fairy-tongue.
He read fairy dreams below,
Legends leaves and flowers must know;
He dream'd fairy dreams, and ye
Changed to fairies, in your glee
Dancing, singing from the tree;
And, awaken'd, fairy-land
Circled childhood's magic wand!
Joy swell'd his heart, joy kiss'd his brow;
I am following funerals now.
Fairy shores from Time depart;
Lost horizons flush my heart.
I am not the child that play'd
Underneath your beechen shade.

" 'Tis the merry child that play'd
Underneath our beechen shade
Years ago; whom all things bright
Loved, made glad with his delight!"

Ah! the bright leaves will not know
That an old man dreams below!

THE OLD MAN AND THE SPRING-LEAVES.

No; they will not hear nor see,
Clapping their hands at finding me,
Singing, dancing from their tree!
Ah! their happy voices steal
Time away: again I feel,
While they sing to me apart,
The lost child come in my heart:
In the enchantment of the Past,
The old man is the child at last!

FIRES IN ILLINOIS.

How bright this wierd autumnal eve—
    While the wild twilight clings around,
Clothing the grasses every-where,
    With scarce a dream of sound!

The high horizon's northern line,
    With many a silent-leaping spire,
Seems a dark shore—a sea of flame—
    Quick, crawling waves of fire!

I stand in dusky solitude,
    October breathing low and chill,
And watch the far-off blaze that leaps
    At the wind's wayward will.

These boundless fields, behold, once more,
    Sea-like in vanish'd summers stir;
From vanish'd autumns comes the Fire—
    A lone, bright harvester!

FIRES IN ILLINOIS.

I see wide terror lit before—
   Wild steeds, fierce herds of bison here,
And, blown before the flying flame,
   The flying-footed deer!

Long trains (with shaken bells, that moved
   Along red twilights sinking slow)
Whose wheels grew weary on their way,
   Far westward, long ago;

Lone wagons bivouack'd in the blaze,
   That, long ago, stream'd wildly past;
Faces from that bright solitude
   In the hot gleam aghast!

A glare of faces like a dream,
   No history after or before,
Inside the horizon with the flames,
   The flames—nobody more!

That vision vanishes in me,
   Sudden and swift and fierce and bright;
Another gentler vision fills
   The solitude, to-night:

FIRES IN ILLINOIS.

The horizon lightens every-where,
　　The sunshine rocks on windy maize;
Hark, every-where are busy men,
　　And children at their plays!

Far church-spires twinkle at the sun,
　　From villages of quiet born,
And, far and near, and every-where,
　　Homes stand amid the corn.

No longer driven by wind, the Fire
　　Makes all the vast horizon glow,
But, numberless as the stars above,
　　The windows shine below!

KING'S TAVERN.

Far-off spires, a mist of silver, shimmer from the far-off town;
Haunting here the dreary turnpike stands the tavern, crumbling down.

Half-a-mile before you pass it, half-a-mile when you are gone,
Like a ghost it comes to meet you, ghost-like still it follows on.

Never more the sign-board, swinging, flaunts its gilded wonder there:
"Philip King"—a dazzled harvest shock'd in western sunset air!

Never, as with nearer tinkle through the dust of long ago,
Creep the Pennsylvania wagons up the twilight—white and slow.

KING'S TAVERN.

With a low, monotonous thunder, yonder flies the
    hurrying train—
Hark, the echoes in the quarry!—in the woodland
    lost again!

Never more the friendly windows, red with warmth
    and Christian light,
Breathe the traveler's benediction to his brethren in
    the night.

Old in name The Haunted Tavern holds the barren
    rise alone—
Standing high in air deserted, ghost-like long itself
    has grown.

Not a pane in any window—many a ragged corner-
    bit:
Boys, the strolling exorcisors, gave the ghost their
    notice—"Quit."

Jamestown-weeds have close invaded, year by year,
    the bar-room door,
Where, within, in damp and silence gleams the lizard
    on the floor.

Through the roof the drear Novembers trickle down
    the midnight slow;
In the Summer's warping sunshine green with moss
    the shingles grow.

Yet in Maying wind the locust, sifting sunny blossom,
    snows,
And the rose-vine still remembers some dear face
    that loved the rose:

Climbing up a Southern casement, looking in neg-
    lected air;
And, in golden honey-weather, careful bees are hum-
    ming there.

In the frozen moon at midnight some have heard,
    when all was still—
Nothing, I know! A ghostly silence keeps the
    tavern on the hill!

ONE OF TWO.

Listen and look! If you listen, you see
A nest with a bird in yonder tree:
Above, in the leaves that glitter with May,
The little half-owner is singing to-day:
"We are very proud, we are rich, and bless'd—
Come and look, if you please, at our nest."

Listen and look! If you look, you hear
The sweetest song you have heard for a year:
Over the nest on the tremulous spray
The little half-owner is singing to-day:
"Soon, in the nest I have asked you to see,
Listen and look for our family!"

AT EVENING.

Hark, out of all the neighboring forest hum
The mingled voices of a myriad things,
(A Sound that half is Silence listening)—
Birds, insects loud with summer, brooks that creep
Slow through the dark and flutter in the light
(As if with prison'd wings) and hurry on,
And the low, lazy turning evermore
Of restless leaves unnumber'd, half-asleep
And yet unsleeping. These, while twilight steals
Great stealthy veils of silence over all,
Feed my old indolence with newer food,
Till, all forgetful of the hour, I see,
Winking above a western cloud, the star
Beloved by lovers and the lover's friend,
And, underneath the boughs and far and near,
The fireflies climbing into dusky air,
Lifting their million stars from grass and weed
Wet with the dew; meanwhile the stars on high
Start one by one—from cells invisible—

AT EVENING.

Visible in the darkness suddenly,
Cotemporaries of the dreamy hour.
Oh, dear to me the coming forth of stars!
After the trivial tumults of the day
They fill the heaven, they hush the earth with awe,
And, when my life is fretted pettily
With transient nothings, it is good, I deem,
From darkling windows to look forth and gaze
At this new blossoming of Eternity
'Twixt each To-morrow and each dead To-day,
Or else with solemn footsteps modulate
To spheral music wander forth and know
Their radiant individualities
And feel their presence newly, hear again
The silence that is God's voice speaking, slow
In starry syllables, for evermore.

A LOST GRAVEYARD.

Near by, a soundless road is seen, o'ergrown with
    grass and brier;
Far off, the highway's signal flies—a hurrying dust
    of fire.

But here, among forgotten graves, in June's delicious
    breath,
I linger where the living loved to dream of lovely
    death.

Worn letters, lit with heavenward thought, these
    crumbled headstones wear;
Fresh flowers (old epitaphs of Love) are fragrant here
    and there.

Years, years ago, these graves were made—no mourn-
    ers come to-day:
Their footsteps vanish'd, one by one, moving the
    other way.

Through the loud world they walk, or lie—like those
    here left at rest—
With two long-folded useless arms on each forgotten
    breast.

THE SIGHT OF ANGELS.

The angels come, the angels go,
   Through open doors of purer air;
Their moving presence oftentimes we know,
   It thrills us every-where.

Sometimes we see them: lo, at night,
   Our eyes were shut but open'd seem:
The darkness breathes a breath of wondrous light,
   And then it was a dream!

TAKING THE NIGHT-TRAIN.

A TREMULOUS word, a lingering hand, the burning
   Of restless passion smouldering—so we part;
Ah, slowly from the dark the world is turning
   When midnight stars shine in a heavy heart.

The streets are lighted, and the myriad faces
   Move through the gaslight, and the homesick feet
Pass by me, homeless; sweet and close embraces
   Charm many a threshold—laughs and kisses sweet.

From great hotels the stranger throng is streaming,
   The hurrying wheels in many a street are loud;
Within the depot, in the gaslight gleaming,
   A glare of faces, stands the waiting crowd.

The whistle screams; the wheels are rumbling slowly,
   The path before us glides into the light:
Behind, the city sinks in silence wholly;
   The panting engine leaps into the night.

I seem to see each street a mystery growing,
  In mist of dreamland—vague, forgotten air:
Does no sweet soul, awaking, feel me going?
  Loves no dear heart, in dreams, to keep me there?

TO THE LARES.

Dear Household Deities, worshipp'd best, we deem,
   With gentle sacrifice of Love alone!
Guardians of Home, who make the hearthstone seem
   Altar and shrine, O make our hearth your own:
Whether the North-wind walls the world away
   With snowy bastions from his frozen lands,
Or Zephyr through our window, day by day,
   Climbs like a child with roses in his hands.

OUTGOING.

A WRATHFUL dust, the spirit of the town,
Follows me, loth to let me free, until
I come to this close lane whose gateway leads
From the low, heated city to the peace,
The high domestic quiet, of the hills.
It is a narrow lane (on either side
A wall: the left of trees—the right of stone,
Roof'd with a hedge) and hides me from the dust
That like a baffled hunter flies beyond,
And welcomes me caressingly with airs
Breathed from a myriad things that hold the breath
Of Summer—weeds that blossom, thorns that flower;
And blesses me with dear and gentle sounds,
(That, mingled, make but quiet felt the more.)
And dewy sights that, seen however oft,
Make the eye always new and can not tire.

At the cool opening of this guardless lane
I think the tender Mother whom I love,

OUTGOING.

Awaiting, whispers with her brooding voice—
Her single, gentle voice that is not heard
By the deaf ear but in the hearkening heart—
" Welcome, O child come back! for all the day
I long'd for thee, my child, and all the day
I dream'd thee lost in yonder barren town,
And sent my messengers to call for thee.
Didst thou not hear a bird beside thy pane
A tender moment—hear but hardly hear?
Didst thou not see a bee that came and went,
Striking thy window—see but hardly see?
Didst thou not feel a wind that turn'd thy page,
Intruding, playful, like a timid child
That fears repulses—feel but hardly feel?
Vexed by the flying leaf, thy blessing held
The breeze that linger'd, but thou didst not come.
I fear for thee, too long in yonder town,
For they forget me there—and wilt not thou?
But see my welcome; see my open door."
So with the dear rebuke I enter in.

The trees in sunset tremble goldenly
Through all their leaves. I wander gladly down
Over a bridge across a troubled rill
(Fluttering from its dark with frighten'd wings);

OUTGOING.

Beyond, the roadway climbs around the hight,
And, look! beneath me, with a music heard
Best in the heart of silence far away,
A falling fleece of silver, shines the dam:
Above, the quiet mirror lets the duck
Float, brooding on its shadow, motionless;
Below, the shallows glitter every-where
As if with shoals of hurrying fish that leap
Over each other noisily in the sun;
And, farther down, the greenly-hidden race
Persuades the seeking eye to wander where,
Gray through the boughs of sycamore and elm,
Tremulous with its myriad-moving wheels,
With sullen thunder stands the busy mill.
While over all, through azure haze adust,
Show the thick spires and the bronz'd marble dome,
Transfigured, far-off, for my memory,
Made beautiful for my forgetfulness.

TO A CHILD.

Oh, while from me, this tender morn, depart
    Dreams vague and vain and wild,
Sing, happy child, and dance into my heart,
    Where I was once a child!

Your eyes they send the butterflies before,
    Your lips they kiss the rose;
O gentle child, Joy opes your morning door—
    Joy kisses your repose!

The fairy Echo-children love you, try
    To steal your loving voice;
Flying you laugh—they, laughing while you fly,
    Gay with your glee rejoice.

Oh, while from me, this tender morn, depart
    Dreams vague and vain and wild,
Play, happy child—sing, dance within my heart,
    Where I will be a child!

IN OCTOBER.

A FLUSH'D cathedral, grand with loneliness,
Gloomy with light and bright with shadow, seems
Thy catholic air, October. Holiest gleams
Alight like angels in each dim recess
Through the stain'd oriels of the east and west;
Thy floors float radiant with flutterings
Of moving shadows, ghosts of glorious wings;
Some organ's soul arises in the breast
Of him who walks thy aisles in revery bound:
The stops of silence tremble into sound.
Lo, Nature brings her dead for burial rite!
Upon thy solemn altars dress'd for Death
She lays her beautiful; the mother's brow
Is bow'd, while for her darling ones she grieves
And o'er their burial breathes her tenderest breath
As o'er their baptism in the April light;
And Autumn, gorgeous preacher, murmurs now
Sermons of dying flowers and falling leaves.

WHITE FROST.

The ghostly Frost is come;
   I feel him in the night;
The breathless Leaves are numb,
   Motionless with affright:
The moon, arisen late and still,
Sees all their faces beaded chill.

The ghostly Frost is here,
   I see him in the night;
Through all the meadows near
   Waver his garments white:
Ha! at our window looking through?
Ah, Frost, this Fire would conquer you!

RESURRECTION.

No season, O friend, may seem
Dearer than that through which I seem'd to go
When the blind Fever, piloting my dream,
    Drifted me to and fro.

I thought that you were lost:
That Light in the dark, or Shadow in the sun,
Had taken you; and helpless I was toss'd—
    Comfortless and undone!

Through all familiar air
That you had breathed I wander'd, but I found
Only your absence in my own despair—
    O never-healing wound!

I could not find you, and
I knew I could not; in a grave you lay
Which I had seen not—over dust and sand
    Blown in a wind's lost way!

RESURRECTION.

    At last you came : behold,
I saw you—from among the dead, I deem'd :
Not free from Death, but bearing as of old
    Your living child, you seem'd.

    White with the following light
Of some new world, whose darkness we but know
Who blindly look, you claim'd your dearest right,
    The mother's place, below.

    A mother's tender heart,
That would not rest, had brought you to your own.
They told me soon again you must depart
    And leave your world alone.

    But still you stay'd and still
You would not go, and Life again at last
Renew'd the warm persuasion of its will,
    Breathing, and held you fast.

    And so my dream was gone.
Lo, I had wander'd almost to that brink
Where the great Darkness standing in the Dawn
    Makes the night-traveler shrink.

RESURRECTION.

'T was I had pass'd away,
And my return that brought you back to me;
I, blind in the mist—you, vanish'd in the day,
    Return'd when I could see.

And, still unwearying, lo!
Though worn and weary, you had trembled near,
O tender watcher, fearing I should go,
    And hoping out your fear!

FORESIGHT OF FATE.

Mother and Child walk in a path of flowers,
Through a bright garden tended by the Hours.

From gentle blossoms, fragrant-hearted there,
Birds, singing, lift the child's heart into air.

Some dreadful House before them grows, unknown:
A ghost of grated casements stares from stone!

Whence came the phantom?—what enchantment wild?
The Mother sees it not nor can the child.

Lo, some lost face, haunting with dreamy glare
The darkness, looking through the darkness there!

How strange if he, lost to himself within,
Were that same child pure as a rose from sin;

And if that face, through those fierce bars aglare,
Saw that same Child cling to that Mother's care!

TO MY BROTHER GUY,

AFTER BUTTERFLIES.

I HAVE watch'd you, little Guy,
Chasing many a butterfly;
I have seen you, boy, by stealth
Strive to pluck the flying wealth
From the blossoms where it grew,
Miracle of a moment new;
I have seen your redden'd face,
Radiant from the bootless chase,
Happy-eyed, with gladness sweet
Laugh away each late defeat;
I have heard your panting heart,
Eager for another start,
Taking newer chances fair
For the elusive flower of air.
I'll not check your joyous chase,
Calling it a useless race;
I will not discourage you
With experience seeming-true,

Showing you with cynic art
Chrysales within my heart;
I 'll not whisper, prophesying,
That the wings are golden, flying—
Dropping all their pretty dust
At the touch of the sweet trust:
Words of warm simplicity,
Fusing cold philosophy,
These would light your lips and brow—
You would chase them anyhow!
Chase them, fleet-foot champion,
Lithe knight-errant of the sun!
Chase the sultry butterflies,
Tropic summers in disguise!
Chase them, while your buoyant feet
Take the heart's ecstatic beat,
While your playmate is the breeze,
While the flowers will hide the bees,
While the birds come singing to you,
While the sunshine gladdens through you!
Butterflies, if caught or not,
Thorough many a gentle spot
They will lead—though vain the chase
It must be in the heaven's face:

For they fly among the flowers,
In bright air, through sunny hours.
Chase them—nothing's dead nor dying:
' Look, your butterflies are flying!

TO ONE IN A DARKENED HOUSE.

O FRIEND, whose loss is mine in part,
    Your grief is mine in part, although
I can not measure in my heart
    The immeasurable woe.

As from a shining window cast
    The fireside's gleam abroad is known,
I knew the brightness that is pass'd—
    Its inner warmth your own.

O vanish'd firelight!—dark, without,
    The late illumined sphere of space;
The warmth within has died about
    Your darken'd heart and face.

If I could hide your gloom with light,
    Or breathe you back the warmth of old—
O vain! I stand in outer night
    And feel you inner cold!

THE BLUE-BIRD'S BURIAL.

I.

AFTER long rains November, in a brief dream of Spring,
Had the tearful eyes of April; some trees were blossoming.

But, long before, October dear April's bloom had bless'd—
Her goldenest hope lay ripen'd upon his swarthy breast.

Hush'd were the noons and leafless the boughs of the cherry tree,
Where the blue-bird sang as prophet, and as preacher humm'd the bee.

Deep in her palace of honey the queen-bee dream'd of Spring,
And moved in winter slumber while the trees were blossoming.

THE BLUE-BIRD'S BURIAL.

And the blue-bird dropp'd—remember, we buried him, darling, found
With the dead leaves, nameless, homeless, and coffinless, on the ground.

We found him and bless'd and buried the prophet of blossom and bee,
With painted leaves for his cover, under his laurel tree:

Saying, "Dear poet and prophet, you bless'd the world, we know;
We give you the poet's guerdon—a grave in Winter snow.

"But bless´d and blessing forever shall be the life you led;
Your breath was a breath of heaven—sleep warm in the Earth's cold bed.

"Forgotten and unremember'd?—remember'd and unforgot!
Your soul shall rise and flutter from many a poet's thought;

"And all the haunted silence deep in the poet's
    breast,
Of Spring and Love and Longing, shall rise with
    wings, express'd.

"Sleep, therefore, April's darling, twin of the violet
    dead,
With the ghost of song in your bosom, the star-
    flower at your head."

II.

You found the star-flower, dearest. O never—though
    all the years
Go out with dirges and darkness and comfortless
    Rachel's tears—

Shall flush the world with fragrance a Spring so lovely
    here
As the dream of Spring, in Autumn, to me you made
    so dear;

When, wandering in the woodland, that gentle day,
    we found
The blue-bird, nameless, homeless, and coffinless, on
    the ground;

THE BLUE-BIRD'S BURIAL.

When, child at heart forever, but woman sweet and brave,
With world-old, tender fancies, you kiss'd the blue-bird's grave.

That night the late, hush'd moonrise came, dusky, large and red:
Jewel'd with frosty jewels it saw November dead.

Within, our fire kept dancing to all sweet dreams and bright:
You said, "I hear the blue-bird sing in my heart to-night."

SLEEP.

The Mist crawls over the River,
  Hiding the shore on either-side,
And, under the veiling Mist forever,
  Neither hear we nor feel we the tide.

But our skiff has the will of the River,
  Though nothing is seen to be pass'd;
Though the Mist may hide it forever, forever
  The current is drawing as fast.

The matins sweet from the far-off town
  Fill the air with their beautiful dream;
The vespers were hushing the twilight down
  When we lost our oars on the stream.

FIRELIGHT ABROAD.

While the wide twilight hushes every thing,
And the unrisen moon's low mystery
Reddens the snow with smother'd Eastern fire,
And, issuing suddenly and bright from heaven,
Hangs yonder star and flutters, look, as bright,
Starting from their close heavens, one by one,
The stars that bless the ended day with peace
Shine steadfastly—the gentler stars of Home!

As one who, thoughtful, gazing at a star,
Marvels what lovelier uplifted lives
Are bound and dwell within its shining air,
By my lone casement so I love to watch
That halo of the fireside shed abroad
Into the world—Home's holy breath of light—
Dreaming of spirits in its inner glow.

There the young bride alights from charmèd air
Into the real air, enchanted still,

Breathing a bower of roses evermore
Over her husband's dusty week-day toil—
Within the harvest lightening the sheaves,
The forge's hammer. There the mother smiles
Her patient days away in daily love,
With gentle lips and tender-touching hands.
There her blithe children, asking for her knees,
(Illumined by the climbing, dancing blaze,)
Cling warm forever, though the years have swept
Even the last spark in ashes, long ago,
From the dear hearthstone, in quick winds of change;
There play their dreams and, lisping dream-like
    prayers,
Send them to Heaven and sleep at Heaven's door.
And there the old, remembering (they who seem
Like helpless trees of some strong forest gone,)
Watch the white ashes crumble from the flame.

If angels come from Heaven to our dim earth,
Thither they come, close visitors unseen,
To find their mortal kindred—as of old—
Troubled and sadden'd at their empty air;
And the three angels born in human hearts—
One playing hide-and-seek, a fickle child;
One, the strong blind believer close to God,

Whispering. through all darkness, "I have light;"
And she, the gentle Warmer of the hearth,
Kindling a flame where the last ember flies—
There in the firelight have their dwelling-place.

The fireside! O, a warm breath fills the name!
The world's first good, the earth's last happiness,
Circle that warmth and breathe that sacred air,
The atmosphere of those soft lights of Home!
We climb for fame, we walk in mountain paths,
But there's a cottage down in yonder vale:
Through the long strife, the storm to take the hour,
Comes the cool wind from the green pathway thither;
Through the white-heated dust a sudden breath
Of the one rose that guards the happy gate;
From the jarr'd street the ever-opening door!

Oh, there we warm our hearts when life is cold,
With memory of days that warm no more!
Circling the firelight from all exile lands,
The anchor that no wind can drift away
Still draws us back. One fireside lights the world!

THE BURIED RING.

Across the door-step, worn and old,
    The new bride, joyous, pass'd to-day;
The gray rooms show'd an artful gold,
    All words were light, all faces gay.

Ah, many years have lived and died
    Since she, the other vanish'd one,
Into that door, a timid bride,
    Bore from the outer world the sun.

O lily, with the rose's glow!
    O rose, the lily's garment clad!—
The rooms were golden long ago,
    All words were blithe, all faces glad.

She wore upon her hand the ring,
    Whose frail and human bond is gone—
A coffin keeps the jealous thing
    Radiant in shut oblivion:

THE BURIED RING.

For she, (beloved, who loved so well,)
    In the last tremors of her breath,
Whisper'd of bands impossible—
    "She would not give her ring to Death."

But he, who holds a newer face
    Close to his breast with eager glow,
Has he forgotton her embrace,
    The first shy maiden's, long ago?

Lo, in a ghostly dream of night,
    A vision, over him she stands,
Her mortal face in heavenlier light,
    With speechless blame but blessing hands!

And, smiling mortal sorrow's pain
    Into immortal peace more deep,
She gives him back her ring again—
    The new bride kisses him from sleep!

THE WHITE LILY.

I DREAM'D and saw a lily in my dream
Of fever'd wakefulness at twilight hour:
Issuing from moonlight grew that blessèd flower
Over my pillow, and the tender gleam
Of its white gentleness, like a soothing stream,
Alighted on me, and I ask'd: "What dower
Of purity is thine, that 'gainst the power
Of all impurity a charm doth seem?"
Transfigured dreadlessly the lily grew
An angel's stature, passing so away.
Then I awoke from fever which had been,
But in that dewy presence could not stay,
And over me you lean'd with holier dew.
Out of your heart had grown the flower within.

TWOFOLD.

If you should vanish, in some lonely place,
And never, never more appear again,
(Though your lost face should float about my brain,
The elusive phantom of a lost embrace,
Out of the mystery of a starless space,)
And I should strive, with long conceptive pain,
Your form so dear from marble to regain,
Or paint the flying memory of your face :
I have not seen you, love, as others deem—
Though stone or color might their semblance give,
I'd watch a child steal shyly from your heart,
To comfort little birds that orphans seem,
Or flowers that need a drop of dew to live,
And this, I think, would baffle subtle art.

ANNIVERSARY.

A MOTHER and a Child, most blessèd sight,
My spirit saw—a pure and holy pair:
The infant open-eyed to morning air
Of its new world, baptized in earthly light;
The Mother with the ecstatic knowledge bright
Of her first motherhood, how gently fair!
Breathing her blissful breath to heaven in prayer,
Keeping her heart so near her new delight!
"Who are you, gentle visions?" then I said—
But these were gone. An Angel came and spoke:
"I am that mother; see my darling's head
I lay upon your bosom." I awoke,
Warm with great tender gratitude, and wept;
Your head was on my bosom while I slept.

AWAKE IN DARKNESS.

Mother, if I could cry from out the night
And you could come (Oh, tearful memory!)
How softly close! to soothe and comfort me,
As when a child awaken'd with affright,
My lips again, as weak and helpless quite,
Would call you, call you, sharp and plaintively—
O vain, vain, vain! Your face I could not see;
Your voice no more would bring my darkness light.
To this shut room, though I should wail and weep,
You would not come to speak one brooding word
And let its comfort warm me into sleep
And leave me dreaming of its comfort heard:
Though all the night to morn at last should creep,
My cry would fail, your answer be deferr'd.

November, 1865.

FOR A GRAVESTONE.

The marble has no speech but that we give,
   And we are dumb, and, speechless, pass away;
The silence in which our affections live
   Holds all we need to speak and can not say.

FOOTSTEPS RETURNING.

RIDING THE HORSE TO MARKET.

OLD miracles happen every day:
That nothing's new in earth or air
It needs no Solomon to say.

Wonderful to the foaling mare,
Was dropp'd a colt of marvelous mettle.
'T was common stock, both dam and sire.
His mane was like a flying fire
When in the unbridled fields he flew,
And some believed him wingéd, too.
The use of such a skittish creature
The village folk could hardly settle;
No rider dared his dangerous back
Save one, a youth, whose mate he seem'd,
Who shunn'd like him the dusty track
With something of a kindred nature—
A boy who did not well but dream'd,
A vagabond with half-shut eyes
Who would not sow in Paradise:

To this one as his rider bow'd
The flying-footed—humble, proud.

'T was plain he was not fit to plow;
For lead or wheel horse on the road
In vain were all attempts to break him—
(To lead right willing he, in truth,
Where none could follow him!) Forsooth,
He balk'd and scorn'd the curse or goad!
"He's good to look at, that is clear,
But little profit anyhow"—
A wrinkle cross'd the farmer's brow—
"And so we'll find him rather dear.
He eats enough—Lord knows—we know!
Here! mount your run-away and go—
To-morrow to the market take him!"

The saying, then the doing: rare
The splendors of the morning show'd,
When ready for the journey there
Stood horse and rider on the road.
"For how much shall I sell him?" said
The youth with pangs of dumb regret:
"As much," the old man hot and red,
"As he will bring and you will get!"

RIDING THE HORSE TO MARKET.

With many a shying make-pretense,
As half in earnest, half in play,
At sliding nothings on the way,
With dainty prance and flame-like bound,
Aërial miles of flying fence,
The dust behind, the wind before,
Townward the horse his rider bore—
Within the air, upon the ground.
At length at day's most noisy heat
They enter'd in the market street;
Among the buyers soon they come,
When—strange that it should happen so,
But so it often happens—lo,
The crowd for praise or blame are dumb:
The merits of the matchless steed,
Unrecognized, have little heed.
At last one cried—"What have we here?
A beggar come to market, clear!"
"What sorry jade is that?" another.
And, strange!—how strange it seem'd, indeed!—
Behold, the wondrous-mettled steed
Has lost the spirit late so plain
In forehead, foot, and mien and mane;
His eyes are dull, his flank no more
Shines with the sunshine, as before;

RIDING THE HORSE TO MARKET.

Their breath his nostrils lose or smother;
His ribs look out, his head is dropp'd,
And, standing lost in public gaze,
His heavenly pulses flutter, stopp'd.
"You want to sell?" a jockey says—
"I think, whatever be your price,
Your buyer makes the sacrifice."
"What are his good points?—let us know them."
"As for his oats—why, let him show them!"
"How many minutes make his mile?"
"I have a dray-horse just his mate!"
"Here, smith, is something for your doing:
What hoofs!—he needs a deal of shoeing!"
And one, a punner, passing late,
"This was the wingéd horse, I vow:
That he's gone up—you see it now!"
Spoke with a self-perceiving smile.
"Speaking of wings," another cries,
"His can't be seen, you see: perhaps
His ears, which can be seen, he flaps
And thinks him flying—from the flies!"

The jockey's scorn, the jeerer's aim,
Meanwhile, the horse and rider both,
In mutual weakness, mutual shame,

RIDING THE HORSE TO MARKET.

Hear—for they must, however loth.
Till—at the last, when, weary grown,
The crowd disperse and leave them there
Unbought within the mart alone—
Awaken'd into buoyant air
From something like a dream of fame,
A poet sees the sultry gleam
Of morning on the city flame,
Far-off, and that deliverance came
Thanks God: the Pegasus he strode
And to the dusty market rode
Was the vague Nothing of his dream!

'TO ———.''

THE CALL OF THE YOUNG MAN.

BELOVED One—whose gentle, floating form
   Visits my dreams in blissful heart and eyes—
Where art thou, Love? My heart is beating warm;
   From dreams alone, I rise!

Long have I known thee: first I saw thy face,
   With laughter ringing through thy girlhood years,
Kissing the Future with a buoyant grace,
   The Past with lighted tears.

Come from my dreaming to my waking heart!
   Awake, within my soul there stands alone
Thy marble soul: in lovely dreams apart,
   Thy sweet heart fills the stone!

Oft I have trembled with a maiden near,
   In the dear dream that thou wast come at last,
Veil'd in her face: oh, empty atmosphere!—
   Those dreams woke in the Past!

"TO ———."

It may be, thou hast ne'er had mortal birth,
   Or childhood's wings to Heaven with thee have
      flown,
My Eve in Paradise! O'er all the Earth
   Must Adam walk alone?

Oh, that thou breathest Earth or Heaven, I know;
   I call, like Orpheus, into shadowy air:
Where art thou, dear? My heart makes answer low—
   Its bridal chamber—"Where?"

Oh, waken in my morning thy pure eyes!
   Thy voice from angel-air of dreams remove.
Sweet Chance! blow those strange seeds of Paradise
   Together, flowering love!

While yet my life is in warm bloom, appear;
   Come ere the first veil from the years depart.
Cottage with thee to me were palace. Dear,
   Thy palace be my heart!

AFTER A WHILE.

On the cold hills the moon lies white,
The ghostly Frost arises bright;
Lost winds wail in the homeless air,
Wandering wearily, every-where:
But, wrapt in dreams of summer mirth,
My cricket sings upon the hearth;
My heart to dreams his dreams beguile—
      "After a while, after a while."

Below the embers ashes darkle;
Above, the lithe flames leap and sparkle,
Dancing to all fantastic forms
Of all that gladdens, cheers and warms;
And, singing to my fancies sweet,
The cricket's spell the flames repeat;
My heart to dreams their dreams beguile—
      "After a while, after a while."

I shut my eyes: my life I see—
Oh, miracle!—a blossoming tree!

AFTER A WHILE.

(The world's sad winds, that cried for rest,
Cradled in blossoms slumber bless'd;)
And from its fragant-hearted May
Some sweet bird joins the cricket's lay;
Oh, tender songs my dreams beguile—
"After a while, after a while."

Winds, rock the world in fairy dreams!
Rise, Frost, and haunt the sleeping streams!
Below the embers ashes darkle;
Above, the lithe flames leap and sparkle;
Sweet bird, bright flames, blithe cricket start
The same dear song of hearth and heart!—
I whisper low, with sigh and smile,
"After a while, after a while."

GENIUS LOCI.

Yes, this is the place where my boyhood
    Saw its beautiful season depart:
The butterfly flutter'd in sunshine,
    The chrysalis lies in my heart!

Still green are the hills in the distance,
    And breathing of Summer the farms,
But the years take the Present forever
    To the Past with their shadowy arms.

I wander in pathways familiar:
    Old faces forget, or are blind;
The footsteps of strangers have trodden
    The footprints I deem'd I would find.

Come back to me, beautiful visions!
    Steal over me, lovelier sky!
With the flower-like soul of my boyhood,
    Blossom, sweet days gone by!

GENIUS LOCI.

My boyhood, come back! In the sunshine
   A hoop is the world of his care:
He gazes at me for a moment,
   And passes away in the air!

Come back! From the school that is ended
   Boy-faces rush joyous and bright:
One, only, among them remembers
   And vanishes into the light!

Come back! With a kite in his heaven
   His heart's happy wings are agleam:
He hearkens my call for a moment,
   And flashes away with my dream!

MELANCHOLY.

Where'er I laugh a buried echo sighs;
   Some coffin full of ashes
Uplifts its dead; a sea-deep sorrow lies
   Under a wave that flashes.

I know not why this moan steals into May,
   To make its joy so hollow;
Some woful hearse keeps hushing through the day—
   My thoughts, dark mourners, follow.

THE WEEK.

Sweet Days, God's daughters, shining o'er the world!
Bright are your feet on the far morning shore,
And, going back to heaven for evermore
Through twilight's dreamy golden gates unfurl'd,
Your footsteps in the dews of evening shine.
A radiant garland round the burning throne,
Guarded with angel wings—a heavenly zone—
Fair are ye all, dear Rays of Light Divine!
Yet fairest is she, the youngest of your name,
In her pure garment of translucent white,
And wearing on her head the halo-light
Brightening till all things near her wear the same:
For—though God loves ye all—when ye are bless'd
His Hand lies on her brow, dear Day of Rest!

FOLDED DOWN.

We read together—here the book.
  (Eyes tender-lidded, drooping, brown!)
The bees were in the roses. Look,
  The leaf is folded down.

It is the story, dear and old,
  Whisper'd forever warm and new:
The world is in its age of gold
  When two are lovers true.

We read together: in the sun
  The brooklet laugh'd through grass and flowers,
All birds were singing; two in one
  We clasp'd the fragrant hours.

The poet's flower—the rose of Love,
  Whence all our costliest honey flows—
Was rooted in the book: above,
  Within our hearts the rose!

The poet's dream—the vision, Love,
   For which all sleeping wake, I deem—
Shadow'd each page with wings: above,
   Within our souls the dream!

We read of Loss that leaves the heart
   A sea-shell on vague shores of fate,
Murmuring, dumb: there walk'd apart
   A maiden desolate.

A sail shone in the horizon's gleam
   Where the moon came—a twilight ghost,
The specter of a vanish'd dream
   That haunts a lonely coast.

What spider from the rose you kiss'd
   Crawl'd, that we read no more that day?
We learn in many an autumn mist
   The brightness of the May.

I turn the page—behold the prize:
   The years like funeral ravens flown.
The sail's reflected in the skies;
   The shell has lost its moan.

FOLDED DOWN.

From shade to sun, to bliss from grief!
    December's warm'd by gracious May;
Oh, fools! we miss'd the golden leaf.
    I read alone to-day.

Is it a memory or a dream?
    (Eyes tender-lidded, drooping, brown!)
In that sad poem, Life, I deem,
    The leaf was folded down.

MIRAGE.

I know the Mirage—the vague, wandering ghost
That haunts the desert's still and barren sand
With the close vision of a lovelier land,
Once blossoming but now forever lost:
It rises to the eyes of men who bear
Hunger of heart and thirst of lip in vain—
Mocking their souls with rest. Behold, how plain!
Taking the breathless sand and boundless air,
It comes up from the horizon, far away:
Lost fountains flutter under beckoning palm,
(Singing, all birds of longing thither start,)
Dear voices rise from homes where children play,
The footsteps lighten, the blest air blows balm.
Then all is sand—within a dreamer's heart!

AN ECHO.

"Come back," I sigh'd—
　　The flower
I dropp'd upon the tide
　Was vanish'd many an hour.
"Come back," the Echo sigh'd

"Come back," I cried—
　　The love,
Flower-like I cast aside,
　An angel bears above.
"Come back," the Echo cried.

SEPTEMBER.

ALL things are full of life this autumn morn;
The hills seem growing under silver cloud;
A fresher spirit in Nature's breast is born;
The woodlands are blowing lustily and loud;
The crows fly, cawing, among the flying leaves;
On sunward-lifted branches struts the jay;
The fluttering brooklet, quick and bright, receives
Bright frosty silverings slow from ledges gray
Of rock in buoyant sunshine glittering out;
Cold apples drop through orchards mellowing;
'Neath forest-caves quick squirrels laugh and shout;
Farms answer farms as through bright morns of
 Spring,
And joy, with dancing pulses full and strong,
Joy, every-where, goes Maying with a song!

FALLEN LEAVES.

I LOVE to steal my way
Through the bright woods, when Autumn's work is done
And through the tree-tops all the dream-like day
    Breathes the soft golden sun;

When all is hush'd and still,
Only a few last leaves, fluttering slow
Down the warm air with ne'er a breeze's will—
    A ghost of sound below;

When naught of song is heard,
Save the jay laughing while all nature grieves,
Or the lone chirp of some forgotten bird
    Among the fallen leaves.

Around me every-where
Lie leaves that trembled green the Summer long,
Holding the rainbow's tears in sunny air,
    And roof'd the Summer's song.

FALLEN LEAVES.

Why shun my steps to tread
These silent hosts that every-where are strown,
As if my feet were walking 'mong the dead,
And I alive alone?

Hast no bright trees, O Past!
Through whose bare boughs, once green, the sunshine grieves?
No hopes that flutter'd in the autumnal blast,
No memories—Fallen Leaves?

TRAVELERS.

We may not stand content: it is our part
To drag slow footsteps after the far sight,
The long endeavor following up the bright
Quick aspiration; there is ceaseless smart
Feeling but cold-hand surety for warm heart
Of all desire; no man may say at night
His goal is reach'd; the hunger for the light
Moves with the star; our thirst will not depart,
Howe'er we drink. 'Tis what before us goes
Keeps us aweary, will not let us lay
Our heads in dreamland, though the enchanted palm
Rise from our desert, though the fountain grows
Up in our path, with slumber's flowering balm:
The soul is o'er the horizon far away.

THE LOVE-LETTER.

I GREET thee, loving letter—
  Unopen'd kiss thee free,
And dream her lips within thee
  Give back the kiss to me!

The fragrant little rose-leaf,
  She sends by thee, is come:
Ah, in her heart was blooming
  The rose she stole it from!

CONFIDANTS.

ALL things that know a lover's heart
   Know the warm secret closed in mine;
From all things eager whispers start—
   "We know, we know it! she is thine."

The swallow seeking southern skies,
   Where some clear summer waters shine,
Circles my tropic dream and flies,
   Singing, "I fly, but she is thine."

Pale flowers, which Autumn's lips have kiss'd,
   Whose far-off May gives back no sign,
Murmur farewell—their souls in mist—
   But smile, in dying, "she is thine."

The cricket from my hearth at night
   Thrills the vague hours with carols fine,
Singing the darkness into light,
   "After a while, and she is thine."

THE BIRDS OF LONGING.

The mournful Birds are flown
  That flutter'd in my breast
Through all the days of Spring,
  And fill'd me with unrest.

The Birds of Longing wild!
  They came in April skies,
Among the blossoming boughs,
  The wingéd prophecies.

Of unknown summer lands
  They sang their haunting dreams—
Poor tropic birds, asleep
  To wake in Arctic gleams!

"Whence came ye, Birds?" I said:
  They sang, "We have no home;
Lost are the nests we loved—
  We long, and long must roam.

"Blown by the vernal winds,
Warm blossom-bearers, we
From soul to soul in Spring
Drift over land and sea."

FIVE YEARS.

HONORS OF WAR.

Wails of slow music move along the street,
Before the slow march of a myriad feet
    Whose mournful echoes come;
Banners are muffled, hiding all their sight
Of sacred stars—the century's dearest light—
    And, muffled, throbs the drum.

Proud is the hearse our Mother gives her son,
On the red altar laid her earliest one!
    Wrapp'd in her holiest pall
He goes: her household guardians follow him;
Eyes with their new heroic tears are dim;
    The stern to-morrows call!

Well might the youth who saw his coffin'd face,
Lying in state within the proudest place,
    Long for a lot so high:
He was the first to leap the treacherous wall;
First in the arms of Death and Fame to fall—
    To live because to die!

Pass on, with wails of music, moving slow,
Thy dark dead-march, O Mother dress'd in woe!
    Lo, many another way
Shall blacken after, many a sacred head
Brightly thy stars shall fold, alive though **dead**,
    From many a funeral day!

Weep, but grow stronger in thy suffering:
From their dead brothers' graves thy sons shall bring
    New life of love for thee:
The long death-marches herald, slow or fast,
The resurrection-hour of men at last
    New-born in Liberty!

WASHINGTON, May, 1861.

THE BALLAD OF A ROSE.

My folded flower last Summer grew
   Sweetly in a glad Southern place;
Its heart was filled with peaceful dew,
   The peaceful sunshine kiss'd its face.

Beside the threshold of a cot
   It knew familiar household ties,
The May's beloved forget-me-not
   To maiden's lips and children's eyes.

Bees climb'd about it; birds above
   Sang in the flush'd year of the rose:
"Our new millennium of Love
   Begins with every May it blows."

Warm cottage-windows murmur'd near
   All music making home so sweet—
The mother's voice divinely dear,
   The lisping tongues, the pattering feet.

THE BALLAD OF A ROSE.

Ah, little rose, another tale
   On your dumb lips has waited long
(Since then your tender lips grew pale)—
   Speak, darling; make your speech my song!

Another tale than cottage peace,
   Than balmy quiet, hovering wings
Of humming-birds and honey-bees,
   And Summer's breath of shining things.

Ah, little rose, your lips are mute:
   Could Fancy give them words to-day,
Such histories would but sadly suit
   Those lips that knew but Love and May!

You woke, one Sabbath, warm and sweet:
   The fields were bright with dewy glow;
The sun smiled o'er the springing wheat,
   And spake, "Let all things lovelier grow!"

What answer rock'd the awaken'd earth,
   Strange echo to that voice divine!
Before the battle's awful birth
   The earth and heaven gave no sign.

THE BALLAD OF A ROSE.

The cannon thunder'd every-where;
    The bomb sprang howling from afar,
A coming earthquake born in air,
    A wingéd hell, a bursting star!

And lo! about the sacred spot
    Where late the doves of home would 'light,
Men red with battle falter'd not
    Though others lay with faces white.

The lowly roof of Love, behold!
    Is rent by shell and cannon-ball;
The rifles flame from casements old;
    By bullets torn the roses fall!

Under the rose-tree where you grew,
    A soldier, dying, look'd and saw
Your face, that only Sabbath knew,
    With Nature's love and Heaven's law.

He heard with ebbing blood and breath,
    At your sweet charm, the thunder cease,
And in that earthquake-hour of Death
    The cannon jarr'd the bells of Peace.

THE BALLAD OF A ROSE.

For while he saw you, tender flower!
   So peaceful in that troubled place,
A tenderer vision touch'd the hour
   And left its halo on his face.

A captain pluck'd you, in the roar
   Of battle, o'er his comrade slain,
And through the fight your beauty bore
   Bloodless upon the bloody plain.

Dear rose, within your folded leaves
   I know what other memory lies;
I hear (or else my ear deceives)
   Your wail of homesick longing rise

"O happy Summer, lost to me!
   O threshold, mine to guard no more!"
You yearn for visits of the bee
   To rose's heart and cottage-door.

Rest in my book, O precious flower!
   And seem—a whitening face above—
The witness in the battle hour
   Of Peace and Home, of God and Love!

1862.

THE OPEN SLAVE-PEN.

We start from sleep in morning's buoyant dawn,
    And find the horror which our sleep oppress'd
A vanish'd darkness, in the daylight gone—
    The nightmare's burthen leaves the stifled breast.

Yet still a presence moves about the brain,
    Some frightful shadow lost in hazy light,
And in the noonday highway comes again.
    The loathsome phantom of the breathless night.

So, while before these hateful doors I stand,
    I feel the burdening darkness which is pass'd,
Or passing surely from the awaken'd land:
    The nightmare clutches me and holds me fast.

Back from the years that seem so long ago
    Return the dark processions which have been;
Lifting again lost manacles of woe
    They enter here—they vanish, going in.

THE OPEN SLAVE-PEN.

Hark to the smother'd murmur of a race
    Within these walls—its helpless wail and moan—
Which, for the ancient shadow on its face,
    Call'd not the morning's new-born light its own!

Imprison'd here, what unforgotten cries
    Of hopeless torture and what sights of woe,
From cotton-field and rice-plantation rise!—
    These walls have heard, and seen, and witness show.

The human drove, the human driver, see!
    Hark, the dread bloodhound in the swamp at bay!
The whipping-post reëchoes agony;
    The slave-mart blackens all the shameful day.

The wife and husband, see, asunder thrust;
    The mother dragg'd from her far children's wail;
The maiden torn from love and given to lust—
    The Human Family in a bill of sale!

All sound reëcho, all sights reäppear:
    (O blindness, deafness! that ye can not be!)
All sounds of woe, that have been heard, I hear;
    All sights of shame, that have been seen, I see!

THE OPEN SLAVE-PEN.

O sounds, be still! O visions, leave the day!—
    What thunder trembled on the sultry air?
What lightnings went upon their breathless way?
    Behold the stricken gates of old despair!

The writing on these barbarous walls was plain;
    The curse has fallen none would understand:
God's deluge ere another happier rain;
    His plow of fire before the reaper's land!

The awful nightmare slips into its night,
    With cannon-flash and noise of hurrying shell:
O prisons, open for returning light,
    The sun is in the world, and all is well!

RIDING TO VOTE.

THE OLD DEMOCRAT IN THE WEST.

Yonder the bleak old Tavern stands—the faded sign before,
That years ago a setting sun and banded harvest bore:
The Tavern stands the same to-day—the sign you look upon
Has glintings of the dazzled sheaves, but nothing of the sun.

In Jackson's days a gay young man, with spirit hale and blithe,
And form like the young hickory, so tough and tall and lithe,
I first remember coming up—we came a wagon-load,
A dozen for Old Hickory—this rough November road.

RIDING TO VOTE.

Ah! forty years—they help a man, you see, in getting gray;
They can not take the manly soul, that makes a man, away!
It's forty years, or near: to-day I go to vote once more;
Here, half a mile away, we see the crowd about the door.

My boys, in Eighteen Sixty—what! my boys? my men, I mean!
(No better men nor braver souls in flesh-and-blood are seen!)
One twenty-six, one twenty-three, rode with their father then:
The ballot-box remembers theirs—my vote I'll try again!

The ballot-box remembers theirs, the country well might know—
Though in a million only two for little seem to go;
But, somehow, when my ticket slipp'd I dream'd of Jackson's day:
The land, I thought, has need of One whose will will find a way!

*He did not waver when the need had call'd for
 steadfast thought—
The word he spoke made plain the deed that lay be-
 hind it wrought;"
And while I mused the Present fell, and, breathing
 back the Past,
Again it seem'd the hale young man his vote for
 Jackson cast!

Thank God it was not lost!—my vote I did not cast
 in vain!
I go alone to drop my vote—the glorious vote again;
Alone—where three together fell but one to-day
 shall fall;
But though I go alone to-day, one voice shall speak
 for all!

For when our men, awaking quick, from hearth and
 threshold came,
Mine did not say, "Another day!" but started like
 a flame;
I'll vote for them as well as me; they died as soldiers can,
But in my vote their voices each shall claim the right
 of man.

RIDING TO VOTE.

The elder left his wife and child—my vote for these
    shall tell;
The younger's sweet-heart has a claim—I'll vote for
    her as well!
Yes! for the myriad speechless tongues, the myriad
    offer'd lives,
The desolation at the heart of orphans and of wives!

I go to give my vote alone—I curse your shameless
    shame
Who fight for traitors here at home in Peace's holy
    name!
I go to give my vote alone, but even while I do,
I vote for dead and living, all—the living dead and
    you!

See yonder tree beside the field, caught in the sud-
    den sough,
How conscious of its strength it leans, how straight
    and steadfast now!
If Lincoln bends (for all, through him, my vote I
    mean to cast)—
What winds have blown! what storms he's known!
    the hickory's straight at last!

NOVEMBER, 1864.

THE UNBENDED BOW.

In some old realm, we read, when war had come,
    The bended bow, a warlike sign, was sent
Across the land—a summoner fierce but dumb;
    When peace return'd the bow was pass'd unbent.

Oh, sacred Land! not many years ago
    (The symbol breathes its meaning evermore),
Thy holy summons, came the bended bow—
    Thy fiery bearers moved from door to door.

Then sprang thy brave from threshold and from hearth;
    Their angry footsteps sounded, moving far,
As when an earthquake moves across the earth;
    Shone on thy hill the flame-lit tents of war.

O tender wife, in all thy weakness stern
    With the great purpose which thy husband drew;
O mother dreaming of thy son's return,
    Strong with the arm whose strength thy country knew;

THE UNBENDED BOW.

O maiden, proud to hold a hero's name
    Close in thy prayerful silence, blameless: lo,
Transfigured in the light of love and fame,
    They come, the bearers of the unbended bow!

"The strife is hush'd, O Land!"—this voice is plain—
    "The bow of Peace is borne from door to door:
May thy dread power be never tried again;
    But let thine arrows shine for evermore."
    1865.

www.ingramcontent.com/pod-product-compliance
Lightning Source LLC
Chambersburg PA
CBHW030403170426
43202CB00010B/1465